100 Ways to Know God Loves Me!

100 Songs to Love Him Back

Created by Stephen Elkins Illustrated by Jeff Ebbeler

THOMAS NELSON
Since 1798

NASHVILLE DALLAS MEXICO CITY RIO DE JANEIRO BEIJING

TABLE OF CONTENTS

God loves me because

TABLE OF CONTENTS

God will answer me,
just as He answered Jeremiah.

He answers my prayers.

JEREMIAH 33

Jeremiah was a great teacher. He taught everyone that God is a listening God. God answers big prayers and little prayers, loud prayers and soft ones. But how do I know God answers my prayers?

Jeremiah 33:3 promises that God will answer every prayer. God's reply may not be heard with our ears and may not be what we expect. But He will hear, and He will answer. So let's do what the Bible says. Let's pray every day. God loves to hear your voice!

I know God loves me because He answers my every prayer.

Call to me and I will answer you.
Jeremiah 33:3

God has given me a place to belong,
just as He did for Adam.

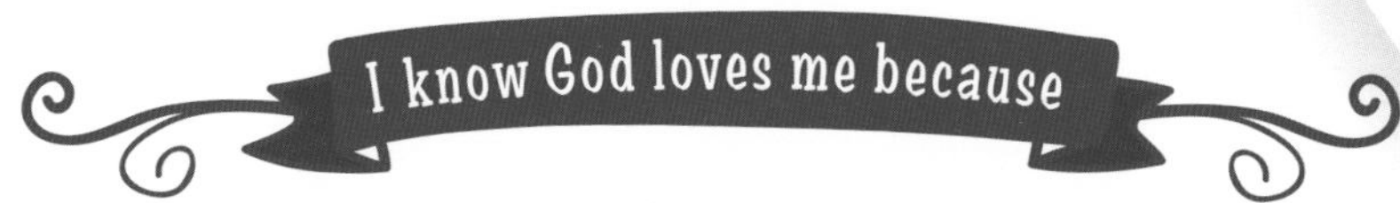

He blessed me with a family.

GENESIS 2-3

Adam was the first person God made. But he was alone. God knew it wasn't good for Adam to be alone. So God created Eve and welcomed the very first family into the garden of Eden. He placed in their hearts a desire to belong.

Psalm 68:6 says that God has given us families so we can belong to each other. A family is a place to grow, a place to love, a place to belong.

I know God loves me because He gave me my very own family.

God sets the lonely in families.
Psalm 68:6

God has given me a home
where I feel safe and loved.

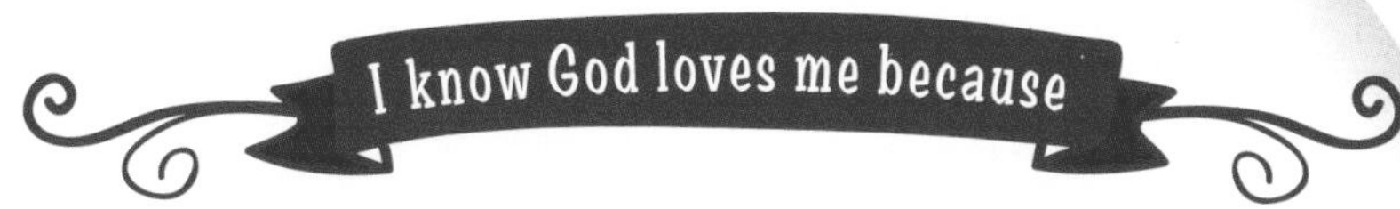

He blessed me with a home.

ISAIAH 32:18

People love going on vacation. Sometimes we can go to the beach; other times we may drive to the mountains and stay in a cabin. It's a lot of fun—for a while. But after a few days, we're ready to go home. Home is the place where we are safe and loved.

Isaiah 32:18 teaches that God gives us homes. He has provided safe, peaceful places where we can rest. Remember, a house is just a building made of wood or bricks. But a home is a place of love where a family dwells. God bless our happy homes!

I know God loves me because He blessed me with a home.

My people will live in peaceful dwelling places, in secure homes, in undisturbed places of rest. Isaiah 32:18

God will give me friends who love me, just as
He gave to the sick man who was brought to Jesus.

He blessed me with friends.

MARK 2:1-12

Jesus was inside a house. Suddenly pieces of mud and straw began to fall to the floor. Four men were lowering their sick friend down through a hole they had made in the roof! Jesus was pleased with the men's love for their friend.

Proverbs 17:17 says that a friend loves at all times. So to be a true friend, we must love . . . no matter what. We must always be willing to help.

I know God loves me because He has given me friends.

A friend loves at all times.
Proverbs 17:17

God blesses me,
just as He blessed Ezekiel.

I know God loves me because

He blesses me.

EZEKIEL 34:25-31

Ezekiel must have loved a rainy day. He knew that rainy days were a blessing from God. Without the rain, there would be no apples or oranges or any other fruit. God showered Ezekiel with many good things we call *blessings*. Does God still send blessings to His people today?

Ezekiel 34:26 gives us a promise. The Lord says, "I will send down showers . . . of blessing." He promises to bless those who love and trust Him. Do you love God? I do too! So the next time a raindrop hits you on the nose, think of God's many blessings.

I know God loves me because He showers me with blessings.

I will send down showers in season; there will be showers of blessing. Ezekiel 34:26

God will call me friend, just as He called Abraham friend, because I will obey Him too.

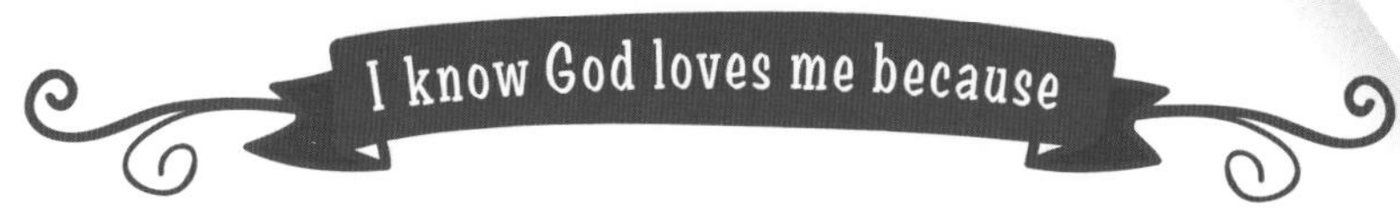

He calls me "friend."

JAMES 2:23

Abraham was called a friend of God. Why? Abraham trusted God. He offered everything he had to God. And because Abraham loved and obeyed Him, God called him "friend." Can I be called a friend of God too?

John 15:15 tells us that Jesus calls us His friends. To be called a friend, we must spend time with someone. We share our feelings with them. We love them. Isn't it nice to know that Jesus calls you friend? Let's spend time with Him.

I know God loves me because He calls me His friend.

I no longer call you servants. . . . I have called you friends.
John 15:15

God calls me His child, just as
He calls all believers His children.

He calls me His child.

1 JOHN 3:1

John was a disciple of Jesus. He tells us something very special about our God: He loves us so much that He calls us His children! John also tells us God loves us with a great love and wants us to love Him too! When you ask Jesus to come into your life, you are saying, "I love You too, God."

In 1 John 3:1 we see that God's love is deeper and wider than any ocean. So there's plenty of love for you and me and the whole wide world. Have you asked Jesus into your life?

I know God loves me because He calls me His child.

How great is the love the Father has lavished on us, that we should be called children of God! 1 John 3:1

When I'm upset, God will calm me, just as
He calmed the disciples and the roaring sea.

He calms me when I'm worried.

MARK 4:35-41

The disciples were so worried! Their boat was caught in a terrible storm. But Jesus lay sound asleep in the back of the boat. Hearing their panic, Jesus awoke and said, "Be still." The storm went away and so did the disciples' fears. Can Jesus calm my worries too?

Mark 4:41 teaches that our God is a mighty God. He's bigger than any problem. When worry and fear come our way, we just need to call the One who can handle it all.

I know God loves me because He calms my worries.

Even the wind and the waves obey him!
Mark 4:41

God will comfort me, just as He did David . . . because I love Him!

He comforts me.

1 SAMUEL 22

Once David was running away from his enemies. He found a dark cave to hide in, but God let David know He was there with him. Will God comfort me too?

Isaiah 49:13 tells us that God will comfort His people. But who are His people? People who love Him, trust Him, and obey Him are God's people.

I know God loves me because He comforts me.

For the Lord comforts his people.
Isaiah 49:13

God will counsel me,
just as He counseled David

I know God loves me because

He counsels me.

1 SAMUEL 18-26

David was tired, weary, and not sure what to do next. King Saul was angry with him. He had even tried to kill him. But David escaped by hiding in different places, such as caves and woods. Four hundred men stood with David, but King Saul had three thousand men! Who would tell David what to do?

In Psalm 16:7 David says, "I will praise the LORD, who counsels me." Yes, our Lord is a wonderful Counselor. So when you don't know what to do, whisper a prayer to the One who does. Ask Him to show you what you should do. His answers are right there in your Bible.

I know God loves me because He counsels me.

I will praise the LORD, who counsels me.
Psalm 16:7

Thank You, Lord, for giving me a wonderful world to enjoy!

I know God loves me because

He created a beautiful world for me.

GENESIS 1

Close your eyes for a moment. What do you see? Nothing! Open them again. Now what do you see? Everything! Did you know that God made everything? He made the tiny little ant and the great big elephant, rainbows above and fish down below. He created an amazing world. And do you know how?

Genesis 1:1 says, "In the beginning God created the heavens and the earth." God said, "Let there be light," and it was so. He spoke and everything came to be! Close your eyes again. Now, let's thank God for the beautiful world He made.

I know God loves me because He created a beautiful world for me.

The earth is the Lord's, and everything in it.
Psalm 24:1

Jesus proved His love by dying
for my sins, just as Romans says.

He died for my sins.

ROMANS 5:6-8

The Bible talks a lot about love. It shows us that love is not just something we say; it's something we do. So what did the Lord do to show that He loves you and me?

Romans 5:8 gives us the answer. He loves us so much that He sent Jesus to die for our sins. You can tell someone you love them, but you really show it by doing something for them. Just think, Jesus came all the way from heaven and died on a cross to show that God loves us.

I know God loves me because He sent Jesus to die for my sins.

God demonstrates his own love for us in this: While we were still sinners, Christ died for us. Romans 5:8

God will discipline me when I disobey,
just as He did Adam and Eve.

I know God loves me because

He disciplines me.

GENESIS 3

Adam and Eve had a choice to make. God had placed the first man and woman in a perfect garden. It had all kinds of trees with good fruit for them to eat. But there was one fruit that God said, "Do not eat." Adam and Eve didn't obey. They ate it anyway. What did God do?

Hebrews 12:6 says that God corrects those He loves. Just like your mom and dad may punish you when you do something wrong, God may punish us to teach us to obey. Because Adam and Eve did not obey, they had to leave their perfect garden home.

I know God loves me because He disciplines me for my own good.

The Lord disciplines those he loves, and he punishes everyone he accepts as a son. Hebrews 12:6

God will encourage me,
just as He did Elijah.

He encourages me.

1 KINGS 19

Elijah was afraid. The mean queen Jezebel had threatened to kill him. When Elijah heard the news, he ran for his life. He slept under a broom tree. But God encouraged Elijah by providing him bread, water, and kind words from an angel.

Romans 15:5 gives us a promise that God will encourage us too. When you are feeling bad, open the Bible. It's full of promises that will cheer you up.

I know God loves me because He encourages me every day.

May the God who gives . . . encouragement give you a spirit of unity.
Romans 15:5

God will fight for me,
just as He fought for Moses.

He fights for me.

EXODUS 14

Moses had led God's people to the shore of the Red Sea. But the enemy was still coming! How would they escape? God told Moses to raise his staff. When Moses did, the sea parted, and all of God's people passed through to safety. Does God still fight for us?

Exodus 14:14 gives us a promise that God will fight for you and me. When we obey Him, He makes sure the enemy doesn't defeat us. He is there to help us win the battle.

I know God loves me because He will fight for me.

The Lord will fight for you.
Exodus 14:14

God forgives me when I admit I've done wrong, just as He forgave David.

Forgive as the Lord Forgives You
CD 1 SONG 16

He forgives me.

2 SAMUEL 12:1-14

David loved the Lord. But one day David did a bad thing. God was not pleased. So He sent Nathan the prophet to David. David confessed his sin to Nathan and to God. What does it mean to confess?

First John 1:9 says that if we confess our sin, God will forgive us. To confess means "to admit." If we know we've done wrong, we admit it to God, and we tell Him we're sorry. If we do this, God will forgive us, just as He forgave David!

I know God loves me because He forgives me when I confess my sins.

If we confess our sins, he is faithful and just and will forgive us our sins. 1 John 1:9

God has given me
hands for work and play.

Let Us Lift Up Our Hands
CD 1 SONG 17

He gave me hands to work and play.

DEUTERONOMY 2:7

Can **you** wiggle your little finger? Go ahead and try! Can you wiggle all your fingers at the same time? Very, very good! Now can you clap your hands? Aren't your hands amazing? God has given us hands for a purpose.

Deuteronomy 2:7 teaches that God blesses the work of our hands. We can use our hands to bounce a ball or play a game. And we can use our hands to work. We can help someone button his coat. God has blessed us with hands to help others.

I know God loves me because He has given me hands.

The Lord your God has blessed you in all the work of your hands.
Deuteronomy 2:7

God gave me life, just as He breathed life into Adam.

He gave me life.

GENESIS 1:26

The book of Genesis tells us how God breathed life into Adam. He became the first human life.

In Job 10:8, 12, Job acknowledges God for giving him life. He said, "Your hands shaped me and made me. . . . You gave me life." Let's do a test. Are you breathing? Is your heart beating? If you answered yes, congratulations! You are alive. Let's thank God for the life He's given us!

I know God loves me because He gave me life.

You gave me life and showed me kindness.
Job 10:12

God helps me believe in myself,
just as He helped Jehoshaphat.

He gives me confidence.

2 CHRONICLES 20

Jehoshaphat had a funny name. But he wasn't laughing the day a great army came against him and God's people. He was afraid that day. He had no confidence in himself or his army. He didn't believe they could win. But he had great confidence in God. So Jehoshaphat prayed. Did God help him? Yes, He did! The Lord defeated Jehoshaphat's enemies.

Psalm 27:3 encourages us. No matter what may be happening around us, we can believe in ourselves because we serve a mighty God. He will fight for us. He is able to do it! Being sure of that is real confidence.

I know God loves me because He gives me confidence.

Though war break out against me, even then will I be confident.

Psalm 27:3

God will direct me, just as He
directed Moses and the people of Israel.

He gives me direction.

EXODUS 13:17-22

The people of Israel left Egypt. They were free from slavery, and they were going home to the promised land! But the trip home that could have taken days took years! With God's guidance, the Israelites finally made it to the promised land after He made them wander in the desert for forty years! Was God giving them bad directions?

Isaiah 48:17 gives us the answer. God wants us to depend on Him, so He leads us in the way we should go. Sometimes the Lord takes us the long way to teach us lessons we need to learn.

I know God loves me because He directs me in the way I should go.

I am the Lord your God, who teaches you what is best for you, who directs you in the way you should go. Isaiah 48:17

God gives me hope, just as He did for
Jeremiah and the people of Israel.

He gives me hope.

JEREMIAH 14:22

Jeremiah taught the people of Israel that they must hope in the Lord. He didn't mean "to wish," like, "I hope I get a bicycle for my birthday." When Jeremiah told Israel to hope in the Lord, he meant that they could expect God to meet their needs.

We should hope in the Lord too! He will meet our needs. Psalm 62:5 promises us rest when we put our hope in God.

I know God loves me because He gives me hope.

Find rest, O my soul, in God alone; my hope comes from him.

Psalm 62:5

God gives me joy,
just as He gave Habakkuk joy.

He gives me joy.

HABAKKUK 3:18

Habakkuk knew the secret. How could he have joy in his heart when his garden didn't grow and there was no food? How could he smile when all his sheep and cattle were gone? How could he still be joyful when bad things were happening?

Habakkuk 3:18 gives us the answer. Habakkuk knew the difference between joy and happiness. Happiness depends on what's happening outside of us. But joy comes from knowing inside that Jesus is my Savior. He loves me and is always with me, no matter what is happening. Now you know the secret!

I know God loves me because He gives me joy.

Yet I will rejoice in the Lord, I will be joyful in God my Savior.
Habakkuk 3:18

God gives me peace
that is not of this world.

I've Got Peace Like a River
CD 1 SONG 23

He gives me peace.

JOHN 14:27

Have you ever wanted a toy so badly that you begged until you got it? Maybe you were happy when you got the toy. But then it breaks or gets old, and you just start asking for a different toy all over again. That toy may have made you happy for a little while, but it didn't give you true peace. You can only find that in one place.

John 14:27 tells us that Jesus promised us peace. Toys can be fun, but the fun always wears off. True peace doesn't come when we get what we want—that's the peace of this world. We have peace when we want what Jesus gives!

I know God loves me because He gives me peace.

My peace I give you. I do not give to you as the world gives. Do not let your hearts be troubled and do not be afraid. John 14:27

God will give me
rest from my troubles.

He gives me rest.

MATTHEW 11:25-28

The Bible teaches that it's good to work. And when we do, we should work at it with all our hearts. But after the work is done, there's a time to come away and rest. Even God rested after He created the world.

In Matthew 11:28 Jesus gives us a promise. He says that when we are tired and worried, we should come to Him. He will give us rest. What a promise!

I know God loves me because He gives me rest.

Come to me, all you who are weary and burdened, and I will give you rest. Matthew 11:28

God will give me sweet sleep,
just as He gave to Jacob.

He gives me sleep.

GENESIS 28

Jacob was very tired. He had traveled a long way. He had no bed, so he slept on the ground. God helped Jacob fall fast asleep even though he had to use a stone for a pillow! Can God help us fall asleep?

As we work for the Lord, He provides us rest. As we sleep, we are refreshed and made ready to face another day. Sleep is very sweet because it is a gift from God!

I know God loves me because He gives me sweet sleep.

The sleep of a laborer is sweet.
Ecclesiastes 5:12

God will give me the knowledge and wisdom
I need, just as He gave to Solomon.

He gives me wisdom.

2 CHRONICLES 1:1-12

To be wise is to make good choices. And good choices always begin with God. When Solomon became king, he knew his people depended on him to make wise choices. So what did he do?

James 1:5 tells us that we can ask God to give us wisdom. Solomon asked God to give him wisdom and knowledge to lead his people. God heard his prayer. Solomon became known as the wisest man who ever lived. You can be wise too. Just ask God.

I know God loves me because He gives me wisdom.

If any of you lacks wisdom, he should ask God . . . and it will be given to him. James 1:5

God has a plan for me, just as He had a plan for Abraham and Jonah.

He has a plan for my life.

GENESIS 12:1-2; JONAH 1:1-2

God had a plan for Abraham. He told Abraham to move to another land. God was planning to build a great nation through him. God also planned for Jonah to go to Nineveh. The people of Nineveh needed to learn to obey God. Does God have a plan for me too? Yes, He does!

Jeremiah 29:11 teaches that God has a very special plan for every one of us. We discover His plan by reading the Bible. As you grow, you can be sure that God will show you His plan for you.

I know God loves me because He has a plan for my life.

"For I know the plans I have for you," declares the Lord, "plans to prosper you and not to harm you, plans to give you hope and a future." Jeremiah 29:11

God has given me a purpose,
just as He gave one to Esther.

He has given me a purpose.

BOOK OF ESTHER

Esther was a Jewish girl who was very pretty and had become queen of Persia. After she found out about a plan to kill God's people, her purpose was clear. She was in just the right place at just the right time to help save them. She went to talk to the king of Persia himself. But would the king listen?

Second Corinthians 5:4-9 teaches us that we have each been created by God for a heavenly purpose. Right now we are in just the right place at just the right time to do what God wants done. God used Esther to save her people. I wonder what God has planned for you?

I know God loves me because He has given me a special purpose.

Now it is God who has made us for this very purpose. . . . So we make it our goal to please him. 2 Corinthians 5:5, 9

God has given me the
gifts of hearing and sight.

He has given me ears to hear and eyes to see. PSALM 94

The Bible teaches us to pray. But sometimes we may wonder, "Does God really hear my prayers? Does God really see me? Does He really hear me?"

Psalm 94:9 tells us that God has given us ears to hear and eyes to see. Without ears we couldn't hear a bird sing or a friend laugh. Without eyes we couldn't see to read a book or work a puzzle. Is it possible that the One who created our eyes and ears cannot see and hear for Himself? Absolutely not! He hears every prayer and sees every need.

I know God loves me because He has given me ears and eyes.

Does he who implanted the ear not hear? Does he who formed the eye not see? Psalm 94:9

God has given me a special gift,
and I should use it to serve Him.

I know God loves me because

He has given me gifts and abilities.

ROMANS 12:4-8

Paul once wrote a letter to the church in Rome. He compared the church to a body. Your body has eyes to see, ears to hear, and legs to walk. Each part of your body does something different, but all the parts work together.

Romans 12:4-8 teaches us that God gives each of us different gifts or abilities to use within His church. Some have the gift of teaching. Others have the gift of encouraging. But we should all use the special abilities God has given us to help one another.

I know God loves me because He has given me gifts and abilities.

We have different gifts, according to the grace given us. If a man's gift is . . . serving, let him serve; if it is teaching, let him teach; if it is encouraging, let him encourage.

Romans 12:6–8

God made this day
so that I can praise Him.

He has given me today!

PSALM 118:24

People can give us a lot of nice things. They can give us a present. They can give us a smile. But there's one thing that I know only God can give. Do you know what that is?

Psalm 118:24 tells us to rejoice because God has given us this day. Our time is very precious. We should use it to love and serve the One who gave us this day! I think there's time right now to praise Him!

I know God loves me because He has given me today.

This is the day the LORD has made; let us rejoice and be glad in it.
Psalm 118:24

God has given me a song to sing.

He has given us music.

PSALM 40:3

When God made Adam and Eve, He gave them each a voice. They could use their voices to talk to each other. They could make happy sounds when they laughed or sad sounds when they cried. But they could do something else with their voices that was very special. Can you guess what it was?

Psalm 40:3 says that God has given us music. We can use our voices to sing a hymn or a praise song to our God. We can say "I love You" or "Thank You" with music. Everything God made is to be used to praise Him—including music! So let's sing a song of praise to our God who gave us music.

I know God loves me because He has given me music.

He put a new song in my mouth, a hymn of praise to our God.
Psalm 40:3

God has given me His holy Word,
just as He did for Timothy and Paul.

He has given us the Bible.

2 TIMOTHY 3:14-17

Timothy received a letter from his friend Paul. In this letter Paul tells Timothy how special the Scriptures are. The Bible is like no other book! And if we read it and do what it says, we will grow in grace and knowledge. But can we be sure the Bible is really God's Word? Yes, we can!

Second Timothy 3:16 tells us that all Scripture is God-breathed. That means that every word we read in the Bible was given by God Himself. We can be sure that if God said it, it is true. So let's read our Bible every day to see what God has to say to us!

I know God loves me because He has given me the Bible.

All Scripture is God-breathed and is useful for teaching, rebuking, correcting and training in righteousness, so that the man of God may be thoroughly equipped for every good work.

2 Timothy 3:16–17

God will heal me, just as
He healed Jairus's daughter.

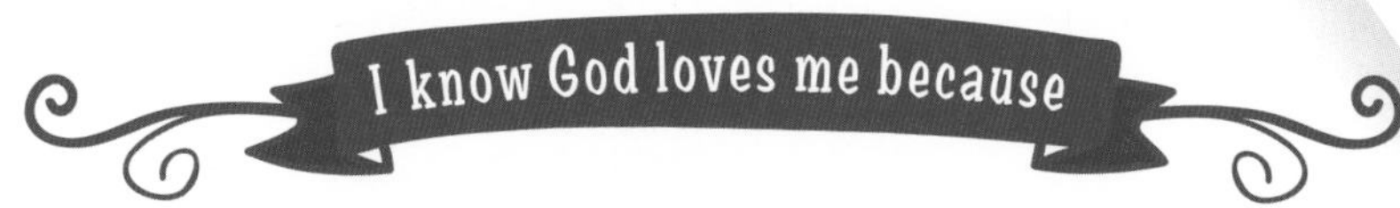

He heals me.

MARK 5:21-24, 35-43

A man named Jairus came to Jesus. He was a synagogue ruler. "My daughter is dying," he said. "I ask You to heal her." Because of the man's faith, Jesus healed the little girl. Does Jesus still heal today?

Jeremiah 30:17 gives us a promise of healing. When you scrape your knee, trust God to heal it. If you are sick and in the hospital, trust God even more!

I know God loves me because He heals me.

I will . . . heal your wounds.
Jeremiah 30:17

God will hear me,
just as He heard Jonah.

He hears my cry.

BOOK OF JONAH

Jonah had been swallowed by a great fish. As he struggled inside the fish's belly, he called out to the Lord. Could God hear his prayers from inside a fish, way under the water?

Jonah 2:2 gives us a promise. When we call out to the Lord, He always hears us . . . no matter where we are! Soon after Jonah called out to the Lord, that fish spit him up on dry land. God had heard his cry. So when you are in trouble, call out to the Lord. He will hear and answer you.

I know God loves me because He hears me when I cry out to Him.

I called for help, and you listened to my cry.
Jonah 2:2

God hears my prayers,
just as He heard Hezekiah's prayer.

He hears my prayers.

2 KINGS 20:1-11

Hezekiah was very sick and dying. He had been a good king, and he loved God. He knew that prayer changes things. So as tears ran down his face, he prayed, "Lord, please heal me."

First Peter 3:12 tells us that God listens. He is paying attention to us and is just waiting to hear our next prayer. God answered Hezekiah. He healed Hezekiah and even added fifteen years to his life. Yes, prayer can really change things because God is listening!

I know God loves me because He listens to my prayers.

For the eyes of the Lord are on the righteous and his ears are attentive to their prayer. 1 Peter 3:12

God will help me make good choices,
just as He helped Joshua.

I know God loves me because

He helps me make good choices.

JOSHUA 24

Joshua had a big decision to make. Would he spend his life seeking God or go with the crowd? God helped Joshua choose the right way. Joshua decided that he and his family would serve the Lord. Does God help us make good choices too?

In Joshua 24:15, we see Joshua choosing to serve the Lord. Serving the Lord isn't always an easy choice, but it is always the right one. What will you decide?

I know God loves me because He helps me make good choices.

This is the way; walk in it.
Isaiah 30:21

God will help me through my troubles, just as He helped Job.

He helps me through trouble.

BOOK OF JOB

Job's life became full of trouble. Though he was a good man, problems still came. But through it all, Job never cursed God for the bad things that happened to him. He still believed God was good.

John 14:1 teaches us that when troubles come we must depend on God to get us through. Remember, bad things happen to everyone. But God can get us through them all.

I know God loves me because He helps me through my troubles.

Do not let your hearts be troubled. Trust in God; trust also in me.

John 14:1

God will help me to be humble,
just as He helped Saul.

He humbles me.

ACTS 9

Saul, also called Paul, did some very mean things to Christians before he became a believer. He was too proud to listen to Jesus. But that was about to change.

Ephesians 4:2 says that Christians should be humble. A person who is humble does not think too highly of himself. He listens to others with respect.

One day Saul was blinded by a light from heaven. He heard a voice saying, "Why are you being mean to Me?" Who was it? It was Jesus! Saul fell to his knees. He listened this time! He knew he had been wrong. Saul called on the name of the Lord and began to serve Him with a humble heart.

I know God loves me because He humbles me.

Be completely humble and gentle.
Ephesians 4:2

God will instruct me,
just as He instructed Moses.

He instructs me.

EXODUS 20

Moses came down from a high mountain with some very special instructions. We call them the Ten Commandments. These commandments were God's instructions for the people of Israel. They also tell us what people who love each other do and don't do.

Psalm 32:8 says that God will instruct us. He tells us what to do and not to do. For example, people who love each other don't steal from each other. People who love each other don't lie to each other. You see, the Ten Commandments are all about love. And that isn't surprising, since God is love!

I know God loves me because He instructs me how to live.

I will instruct you and teach you in the way you should go.
Psalm 32:8

The Lord will be with me, just as
He was with David when he faced Goliath.

He is always with me.

1 SAMUEL 17

Goliath was over nine feet tall! His big armor glistened in the sunlight. Even the spear he carried was probably taller than David, the boy who stood before him. David's small sling was in his hand as he shouted, "You come against me with a sword, but I come against you in the name of the Lord." Why was David so sure he could beat that big giant?

In Psalm 23:4 we read a promise that David believed. God will always be with you. It doesn't matter where you are or what danger is before you. He will be with you always. And no matter how big your trouble, your "Goliath," may be, you can defeat it in the name of the Lord!

I know God loves me because He is always with me.

I will fear no evil, for you are with me.
Psalm 23:4

Jesus is coming for me, just as
the angels told the disciples He would.

He is coming again for me.

ACTS 1:6-11

Jesus' work on earth was done. He rose up through a cloud and into heaven. As the disciples watched, two angels suddenly appeared. They announced that Jesus would come again. Why is Jesus coming again?

Acts 1:11 gives us a promise. One day Jesus will come again. He will come with the clouds, and every eye will see Him. But this time He is coming to gather all those who have believed in Him. That's you and me!

I know God loves me because Jesus is coming again to take me home to heaven.

Jesus . . . will come back in the same way you have seen him go into heaven. Acts 1:11

God is faithful.
I know I can depend on Him.

I know God loves me because

He is faithful.

MARK 11:1-7

Jesus needed a donkey. So He instructed His disciples to go and get one. Jesus expected them to be faithful. He depended on them to do what He asked.

Second Thessalonians 3:3 tells us that the Lord is faithful. That means we can depend on Him. We can depend on Him to strengthen and protect us, just as the Bible says. A faithful friend is a dependable friend. It's good to know our God is faithful.

I know God loves me because He is faithful.

But the Lord is faithful, and he will strengthen and protect you from the evil one. 2 Thessalonians 3:3

God is good to me, just as He was good
to Hannah when He gave her a son.

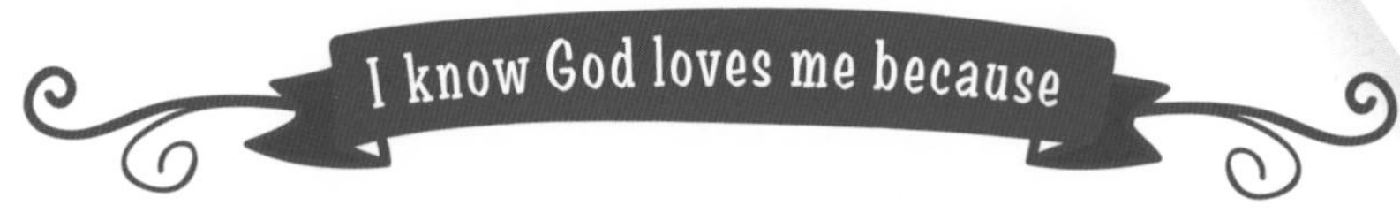

He is good to me.

1 SAMUEL 1

Hannah was very sad. She had waited so long. It seemed like God was far away and wasn't listening to her prayers. Year after year she pleaded, "Bless me with a child, LORD!" And finally, something wonderful happened!

Lamentations 3:25 says that God is good to those who trust in Him. Hannah did! That's why she kept praying. God answered her prayers. And that's why she had a little baby boy and named him Samuel, which means "heard by God." God is good!

I know God loves me because He is good to me.

The LORD is good to those whose hope is in him.
Lamentations 3:25

God will show kindness to me, just
as He did to David and Mephibosheth.

He is kind to me.

2 SAMUEL 9

Mephibosheth was the grandson of King Saul. When David became king, he sent for Mephibosheth. David knew that God had been kind to him, and he wanted to show kindness to Saul's grandson. He gave Mephibosheth a royal place and workers for his land. How did David learn to be kind?

Exodus 1:20 tells us that God is kind. And when we accept God's kindness, we should pass it on—just like David did!

I know God loves me because He shows kindness to me.

So God was kind. Exodus 1:20

God is on my side,
just as He was with Joshua.

I know God loves me because

He is on my side.

JOSHUA 5:13-6:27

As Joshua and his army came near to the city of Jericho, he met a man holding a sword. Joshua asked, "Are you for us or for our enemies?" The man said, "Neither," and told Joshua that he had come as commander of the Lord's army. Had he come to fight for Joshua or against him?

Romans 8:31 tells us that if God is for us, no one can defeat us. If you are "for" someone, that means you are on his side; you are his friend. The heavenly messenger told Joshua that he was on the right side—God's side!

I know God loves me because He is on my side.

If God is for us, who can be against us?
Romans 8:31

God will be patient with me,
just as He was patient with Paul.

I know God loves me because

He is patient with me.

1 THESSALONIANS 5

God waited patiently for Paul to come to Christ. Paul later sent a letter to a church asking them to be patient with everyone. People don't always come to Jesus the first time you ask. We must wait for others, just as Jesus waits for us.

First Thessalonians 5:14 asks us to be patient. When people see us kindly and quietly waiting, they will learn to do the same! Nobody likes to wait, but we can learn to be patient. Be patient with your brothers and sisters, just as God is patient with you. God will be pleased!

I know God loves me because He is always patient.

He is patient with you.
2 Peter 3:9

Jesus is preparing a home for me in heaven, just as He told His disciples.

The Kingdom of Heaven CD 1 SONG 48

He is preparing a place for me.

JOHN 14:1-3

Jesus had twelve very special friends. They were sometimes called His disciples. They helped Jesus do His work. One day the disciples were feeling sad. So Jesus gave them some very good news.

John 14:1-3 tells us what Jesus said to them. "Don't be troubled," He said. "I am going to prepare a place for you in heaven. Then I will come back and take you to your new heavenly home." And the promise Jesus made wasn't just for His disciples. He is preparing a home for each and every one who trusts in Him!

I know God loves me because He is preparing a home for me in heaven.

In my Father's house are many rooms; if it were not so, I would have told you. I am going there to prepare a place for you. John 14:2

God will keep His promises to
me, just as He did for Abraham.

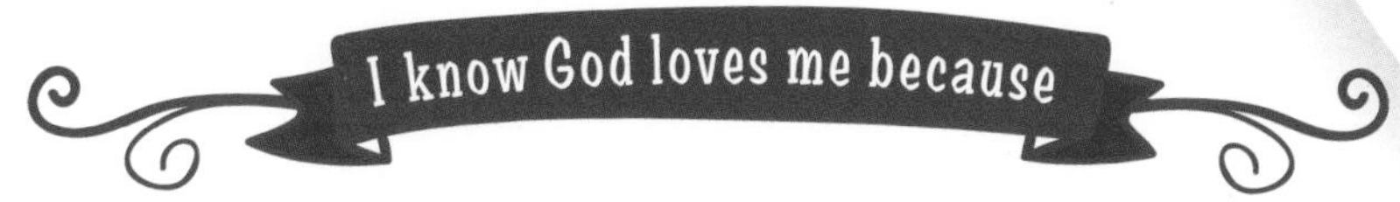

He keeps His promises.

GENESIS 15, 17, 21

God took Abraham outside under the night sky. As Abraham looked up into the heavens, he heard the voice of God saying, "Abraham, one day your family will number more than the stars." And God kept His word. He always does!

Psalm 145:13 says the Lord is faithful to keep every promise. And the Bible is full of promises, big and small.

I know God loves me because He keeps His promises to me.

The LORD is faithful to all his promises.
Psalm 145:13

God will look after me,
just as He looked after Joseph.

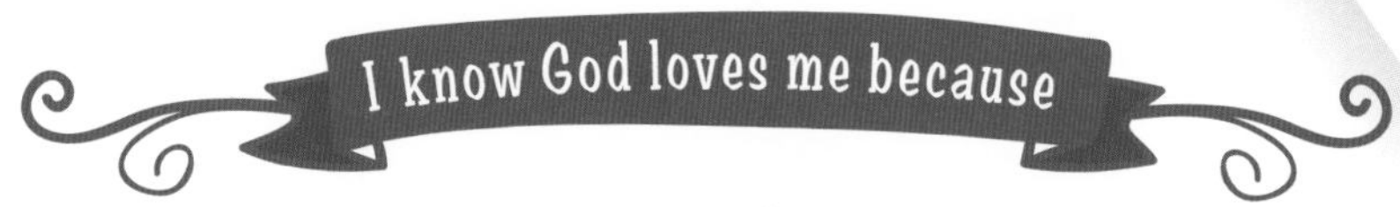

He keeps me from harm.

GENESIS 37

Joseph's brothers had been so unkind. When he was just a boy, Joseph's brothers sold him as a slave, and he had to live in a land far away from his family! Who would watch over him?

Psalm 121:5 tells us that the Lord is watching over each of us. Even though Joseph's brothers had tried to hurt him, God kept Joseph safe. God had a special plan for Joseph to one day help the brothers who had harmed him. God will watch over us too.

I know God loves me because He will keep me from harm.

The Lord will keep you from all harm.
Psalm 121:7

God will keep my family safe,
just as He kept Rahab's family safe.

O Lord, My Lord (You Will Keep Us Safe)
CD 2 SONG 1

He keeps my family safe.

JOSHUA 2

Rahab had heard about the mighty God of Israel. She believed in His power. She knew God would help His people. He would give them the land where she lived, called Canaan. So when the king of Jericho sent men to capture the two spies from Israel, Rahab hid them on her roof. She promised them a way of escape if they would keep her family safe. What happened to Rahab when the battle was fought?

Proverbs 29:25 says that whoever trusts in the Lord is kept safe. When the battle came, Rahab and everyone in her house were saved. We can trust in the Lord to protect us too!

I know God loves me because He keeps my family safe.

Whoever trusts in the Lord is kept safe.
Proverbs 29:25

God knows my needs before I do,
so I will not worry about tomorrow.

He knows my needs before I ask.

MATTHEW 6:8

It may surprise you to know that God is never surprised! He knows what will happen tomorrow before the sun even comes up. In fact, God knows everything. He knows you need a coat before the snow falls. He knows you need a bed before you get sleepy. He knows you need a friend before you get lonely.

Matthew 6:8 says that God knows our needs before we even ask. What an amazing God He is! He knows everything, even the things we won't know until tomorrow.

I know God loves me because He understands my needs.

Your Father knows what you need before you ask him.
Matthew 6:8

The Good Shepherd leads me,
and like a sheep I will follow.

He leads me.

JOHN 10:3, 14

People are very much like sheep. And like sheep, we would get lost without our Shepherd. Jesus said a good shepherd leads his sheep. Does Jesus lead me too?

In John 10:14 Jesus called Himself the Good Shepherd. He is "good" because He loves us and always does what is best for us. He is called "Shepherd" because He guides us and watches over us—just like a shepherd who guides and watches over his sheep. He said the sheep will recognize their shepherd's voice and follow.

I know God loves me because He leads me.

He calls his own sheep by name and leads them out.

John 10:3

Jesus loves me, just as He
loved the children who came to Him.

He loves all the children!

MATTHEW 19:13-15

Have **you** ever sung, "Jesus loves the little children, all the children of the world"? It's true, you know. There's not a boy or girl anywhere in the world that Jesus doesn't love. You know how I know? Because of what Jesus said!

In Matthew 19, Jesus takes time to bless kids. One day His disciples tried to keep the children away from Jesus. But He said, "Let the little children come to Me." Yes, Jesus loves the little children. And He loves you too!

I know God loves me because He loves all of His children!

Jesus said, "Let the little children come to me, and do not hinder them, for the kingdom of heaven belongs to such as these." Matthew 19:14

God has made me part of His family,
just like the believers in Galatia.

He made me part of His family.

GALATIANS 6

Paul wrote a letter to the believers in Galatia. Though he probably hadn't met all of them, he still called them "brothers" and "sisters." Why would Paul do that?

Galatians 6:10 tells us that there is a family of believers. When we come to know Jesus as Lord and Savior, we become part of God's family. God becomes our Father, and we join a great big family of believers. And just like a family, we share a name—the name of Jesus Christ. We are all called Christians!

I know God loves me because He made me part of His family.

Let us do good to all people, especially to those who belong to the family of believers. Galatians 6:10

God made me like no one else.

He made me Special.

PSALM 139:14

What makes YOU special? Is it the color of your eyes or the shape of your nose? Maybe it's the freckles on your cheeks or your funny little toes. One thing is for sure: God made you special.

Psalm 139:14 teaches that you are fearfully and wonderfully made. You are amazing because God created you, and there is no one quite like you. Everyone may have two eyes and two ears, but there is only one you!

I know God loves me because He made me special.

I praise you because I am fearfully and wonderfully made.
Psalm 139:14

God made all the
animals with a purpose.

All Creatures of Our God and King
CD 2 SONG 7

He made all the animals.

GENESIS 1

God created all kinds of animals. Some quack, some eat hay, some moo, and some neigh! Each one is special because God made it! We enjoy having dogs, cats, talking parrots, and other animals as pets. But animals are not only pets, they are on the earth to help us.

Genesis 1:26 says that people are to rule over the animals. We should care for them wisely and not misuse them. Cows give us milk. Chickens give us eggs. Horses can carry heavy loads for us. So no matter what kind of animal you see, you can be sure it has a purpose.

I know God loves me because He created all the animals.

God made the wild animals . . . the livestock . . . and all the creatures that move along the ground. . . . And God saw that it was good. Genesis 1:25

God makes all things possible for me, just
as He did for Mary, Martha, and Lazarus!

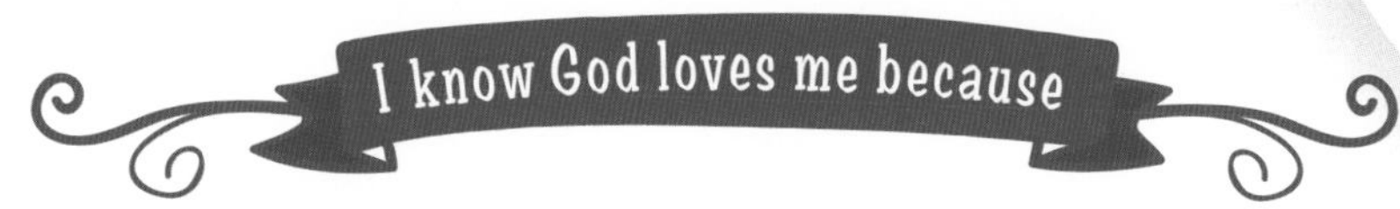

He makes all things possible.

JOHN 11:1-44

Mary and Martha sent a message to Jesus. Their brother, Lazarus, was sick. They knew Jesus could make him well. But Jesus didn't come quickly. As they were waiting, Lazarus died. He had been dead for four days when Jesus finally arrived. Jesus went to the tomb where Lazarus was buried. He shouted, "Lazarus, come out!"
Could Jesus make Lazarus live again?

Matthew 19:26 says that nothing is impossible with God. Lazarus walked out of the tomb alive! Jesus showed us that God can do anything—even the impossible.

I know God loves me because He makes all things possible.

With man this is impossible, but with God all things are possible.
Matthew 19:26

God will make me glad,
just as He made David glad.

He makes me glad.

PSALM 92

David knew that God created the heavens and the earth. When he saw all the things God had made, he wrote songs to praise Him. And as he thought about all God had done, his heart was made glad. Who can be sad knowing God loves us?

In Psalm 92:4 David thanks the Lord. "You make me glad," he says. When we look at the beautiful world God has made, we can say God has made us happy.

I know God loves me because He gives me a reason to be glad.

For you make me glad by your deeds, O LORD.
Psalm 92:4

God makes me laugh, just as Sarah did.

He makes me laugh.

GENESIS 18

Sarah laughed to herself. She had heard God say that she would have a baby. It was very funny. How could a ninety-year-old woman have a baby? It might have been funny if God hadn't promised it would happen. So why was Sarah laughing?

Ecclesiastes 3:4 tells us that there is a time to laugh and a time to cry. Sarah thought God's promise was not possible. But one year later, Sarah held her new baby boy in her arms. At last she was a mother! Now Sarah laughed because she was so happy!

I know God loves me because He makes me laugh.

There is a time for everything . . . a time to weep and a time to laugh.
Ecclesiastes 3:1, 4

God will never forget me, because my
name is written on the palm of His hand.

He never forgets me.

ISAIAH 49

The people of Israel were tired and confused. "God has forgotten us!" they cried. Had God really forgotten them? Of course not! So God gave Isaiah a message for Israel. It was a comforting message: "God will never forget you! As a mother could never forget her baby, God could never forget you."

Isaiah 49:15-16 contains a promise. The names of those who live for God are written on the palms of God's hands. We will never be forgotten! Remember, this one thing our God cannot do: He cannot break a promise. And He has promised in His Word that He will never forget you.

I know God loves me because He has promised never to forget me.

I will not forget you!
Isaiah 49:15

God will lift me up when I fall and don't believe in Him like I should, just as He lifted Peter.

He picks me up when I fall.

LUKE 22:54-62

Peter had fallen into sin. Peter had been a brave follower of Jesus, but he was not tonight. He was afraid. Jesus had been arrested. So Peter told some people he didn't know Jesus. That was a lie. He had fallen into sin, but what could he do?

Psalm 145:14 gives us all hope. Everyone falls into sin, but God has promised to pick us up if we call to Him. He takes care of all who love Him. He forgives us for what we have done wrong. And when God forgives us, He makes us new again!

I know God loves me because He promises to pick me up when I fall.

The Lord upholds all those who fall and lifts up all who are bowed down. Psalm 145:14

God will give me eternal life,
just as He promised.

When We All Get to Heaven CD 2 SONG 13

He promises me eternal life.

JAMES 4:13-16

Have **you** ever seen a mist cover the ground on a chilly morning? The mist soon disappears as the sun warms the earth. It only lasts a short time, then poof, it's gone! James tells us that our life on this earth is like a mist; it only lasts a short time. But God promises us another kind of life. It's called *eternal life.* What is eternal life?

John 3:36 tells us that whoever believes in Jesus will have eternal life. Here on earth, life will come to an end one day. But in heaven, life with Jesus never comes to an end. It goes on and on, forever; it's eternal.

I know God loves me because He gives me eternal life.

Whoever believes in the Son has eternal life.

John 3:36

God will show me the way,
just as He showed Isaiah.

I know God loves me because

He promises to guide me.

ISAIAH 58

Isaiah was a very wise man. He preached with great power. With patience and love, Isaiah led the people of Israel back to the Lord. But like you and me, Isaiah surely had days when he didn't know what to do. Isaiah gave guidance to the people of Israel, but who guided him?

Isaiah 58:11 says that God promises to lead us and take care of all our needs. No matter where we are, God is always there to show us the way. Isaiah depended on the Lord to direct his ways.

I know God loves me because He guides me in the way I should go.

The Lord will guide you always.
Isaiah 58:11

God will help me,
just as He helped Paul.

My Help Comes from the Lord
CD 2 SONG 15

He promises to help me.

2 CORINTHIANS 11-12

Paul was no stranger to danger. Three times he was shipwrecked, and he often went hungry. He was beaten, stoned, and left to die. Many people looked to Paul when they were afraid and confused. Yet who could Paul turn to when he was afraid?

Psalm 46:1 promises that God is our strength in times of trouble. God is always there to help. Though Paul helped so many people in their walk with the Lord, God was always there to help Paul.

I know God loves me because He helps me in all I do.

God is our refuge and strength, an ever-present help in trouble.

Psalm 46:1

God watches over me,
just as He watched over David.

He promises to watch over me.

PSALM 23

David was a shepherd boy. He spent many nights alone on a hillside watching over his sheep. The sheep depended on David to keep them safe. But who would watch over David and keep him safe?

Psalm 23 gives us a wonderful promise. Even though David would walk through the valley of the shadow of death, he said he would fear no evil, because God was with him. The sheep depended on David, and David depended on God!

I know God loves me because He watches over me.

For the Lord watches over the way of the righteous.
Psalm 1:6

God will protect me,
just as He protected baby Moses.

He protects me.

EXODUS 2:1-10

A little baby boy was in danger. His name was Moses. His mother hid him for three months to protect him from the evil king of Egypt. When she could no longer keep him hidden, she placed him in a floating basket. She set the basket among the tall grass along the bank of the river. Who would protect baby Moses now?

Psalm 32:7 gives us a promise. God will protect us from trouble. He helped baby Moses to safety. And He watches over us when moms and dads cannot. He surrounds us like a shield and keeps us from danger. God is like a very special hiding place where we are safe!

I know God loves me because He protects me.

You are my hiding place; you will protect me from trouble and surround me with songs of deliverance. Psalm 32:7

God gives me clothing to wear,
just as He clothes the flowers.

Isn't He Wonderful? CD 2 SONG 18

He provides clothes for me.

MATTHEW 6:28-33

Have you ever been to a mall to shop for clothes? It's amazing how many different colors, styles, and fabrics there are to choose from. There are shirts in every color of the rainbow, and pants to fit every size. There are sweaters to keep warm and bathing suits for a cool dip in the pool. There are even dresses with shoes to match!

Matthew 6:28-33 tells us that even our clothes come from God. He knows we need to stay warm and dry, so He provides us with clothes, just as He provides for the beautiful flowers. So the next time you worry about what to wear, just remember the flowers and thank God for your clothes!

I know God loves me because He provides clothes for me.

See how the lilies of the field grow. They do not labor or spin. Yet . . . not even Solomon in all his splendor was dressed like one of these. Matthew 6:28–29

God gives me everything I need,
just as Philippians promises.

He provides everything I need.

2 KINGS 4:1-7

Can **you** think of some things we need every day? We need food, and God supplies it. You may ask, "Doesn't food come from the grocery store?" Yes, but without the rain and seeds that God provides, the stores would be empty.

Philippians 4:19 says that God meets all our needs. So whether it is water to drink, food to eat, or somewhere to sleep—even the air we breathe—God meets our needs. So take a deep breath. Now breathe out. Let's say, "Thank You, God, for meeting my needs."

I know God loves me because He provides everything I need.

And my God will meet all your needs according to his glorious riches in Christ Jesus. Philippians 4:19

God gives me food to eat, just as He
did for Moses and the people of Israel.

He provides food for me.

EXODUS 16:4, 31

Moses kept telling Pharaoh, "Let my people go." Finally, Pharaoh listened and set them free! The people of Israel left Egypt and started across a desert toward the promised land. Yes, they were free, but what would they eat in the desert?

Exodus 16:4 says that God gave them food. Each morning they gathered white flakes that appeared on the ground. They made the flakes into bread and called it *manna*. It tasted like wafers made with honey. Yum! God gave His people this food for forty years.

I know God loves me because He provides food for me.

He provides food for those who fear him.
Psalm 111:5

God gives light to all the world.

Heavenly Sunlight
CD 2 SONG 21

He provides us with light.

GENESIS 1

God made everything that gives us light. He made moonlight to brighten the night. With a word He made millions of stars twinkle in the sky. Even the smallest flame on the tip of a candle comes from God. But there's something that shines even brighter!

Genesis 1:16 says that on the fourth day of Creation God made sunshine. Without sunshine we couldn't see all the wonderful things God has made. The world would be so dark without the sun. But did you know there's Someone who shines with more glory than sunshine? Yes, it's Jesus! He's the Light of the world!

I know God loves me because He provides us with light.

God made . . . the greater light to govern the day.
Genesis 1:16

God rejoices with heavenly
songs because of me.

He rejoices over me with singing.

ZEPHANIAH 3:17

Zephaniah wrote a very small book with a great big message. It says that God protects His people from enemies. It says that God calms us down when we are afraid. And it says that God loves us so much that He sings with joy because of us!

Zephaniah 3:17 says that God rejoices over us with singing. That's easy to believe. After all, God created music, so why wouldn't He sing? Isn't it wonderful to know that God loves you so much, He sings about you?

I know God loves me because He rejoices over me with singing.

The Lord your God . . . will rejoice over you with singing.
Zephaniah 3:17

God will rescue me, just as He did
Shadrach, Meshach, and Abednego.

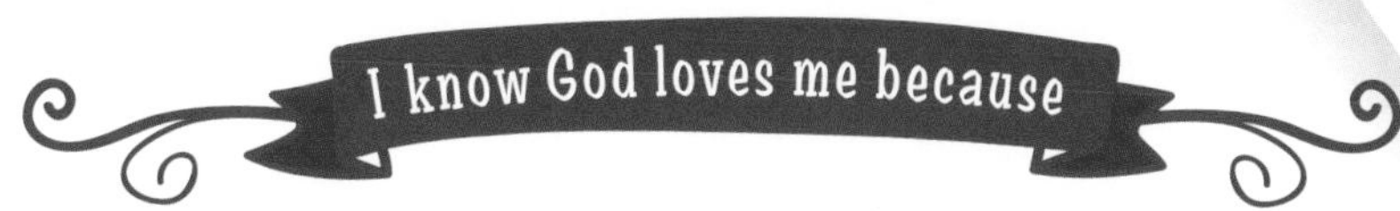

He rescues me.

DANIEL 3

Shadrach, Meshach, and Abednego stood before a giant fiery furnace. They would not bow down to a false god. "Our God is able to save us," they told the king. "Throw them into the furnace!" ordered the king. Would God rescue them?

Our God is able to rescue His people from danger. Shadrach, Meshach, and Abednego were thrown into the fire, but they were not burned! God protects those who are faithful to Him.

I know God loves me because He rescues those who love Him.

The Lord knows how to rescue godly men from trials.
2 Peter 2:9

God will restore me, just as
He restored the man's crippled hand.

He restores my soul.

MATTHEW 12:9-14

As Jesus entered a place of worship, He saw a man with a crippled hand. Jesus told the man to stretch out his hand. As the man did what Jesus said, the crippled hand began to move, just like his other hand. It was made like new again. It was restored!

Psalm 23:3 teaches us that God not only can restore a hand, He can restore a broken heart. He can make it like new. The Lord can remove any hurt or pain and replace it with hope and love. He can restore a broken hand, and He can restore a broken heart!

I know God loves me because He restores me.

He makes me lie down in green pastures, he leads me beside quiet waters, he restores my soul. Psalm 23:2–3

When I call on Him,
God will save my soul.

I know God loves me because

He saves my soul.

ROMANS 10:13

Every apple has three main parts. You can see the skin on the outside. The sweet part is in the middle. And the seeds are deep in the core. People are sort of like that too. We have a body that you can see. We have a mind on the inside. And we have a soul deep inside that lives forever.

The Bible tells us that Jesus came to save our souls. Our body grows old. It may become sick and die. The mind grows old too. But our soul never dies. It lives forever. Whoever chooses to call on the Lord will live forever in heaven. That's what it means to be saved. So choose Jesus!

I know God loves me because He saves my soul.

"Everyone who calls on the name of the Lord will be saved."
Romans 10:13

God sends the rain as a
blessing to those He loves.

He sends rain.

LEVITICUS 26:4

Do you know which raindrop is the most exciting? It's the first one to hit the farmer's nose. That is the first raindrop that tells the farmer that God has heard his prayers. The rain is coming! Why is that so important?

Leviticus 26:4 teaches that rain is a blessing from God. Without the rain, the flowers, trees, and plants cannot grow. So when the Lord sends the rain, He sends a great big, wonderful, wet blessing.

I know God loves me because He sends the rain.

I will send you rain in its season, and the ground will yield its crops and the trees of the field their fruit. Leviticus 26:4

God puts His Holy
Spirit in my heart.

He Sent His Holy Spirit.

EZEKIEL 36:27

Our eyes are amazing. They can see a bright light or a tiny candle. They can see big elephants and tiny ants. But there are some things our eyes can't see, like the wind. You can feel the wind blow, but you can't see it. God is like that.

Ezekiel 36:27 teaches us that God's Holy Spirit is there to guide His people. The Holy Spirit helps us live for Jesus. Our eyes can't see Him, but like the wind, He is there.

I know God loves me because He sent His Holy Spirit.

And I will put my Spirit in you and move you to follow my decrees and be careful to keep my laws. Ezekiel 36:27

God sent Jesus to die for me
so that my sins could be forgiven.

I've Got Good News
CD 2 SONG 28

He sent Jesus to die for me.

JOHN 3:16

God had a plan. It seemed a bit unusual, but His plans are not like ours. John tells us about it. God loves you and me. And He wants us to live with Him forever in heaven. But there is a problem. Heaven is a perfect place, and none of us is perfect. So how will we ever get there?

John 3:16 gives us the plan. God sent Jesus into this world to take away our sins. If we trust Him, we can live in God's world forever. His world is called heaven. Trusting Jesus makes us perfect in God's sight. A plan that makes us perfect—what a perfect plan!

I know God loves me because He sent His Son to die for my sins.

For God so loved the world that he gave his one and only Son, that whoever believes in him shall not perish but have eternal life. John 3:16

God has set me apart
as one of His children.

He sets me apart as His own.

MARK 1:1-8

John the Baptist didn't look like most people. He wore funny clothes made of camel's hair. He didn't eat like most people either. He ate locusts and wild honey. He didn't even live in a house like most people. His home was in the desert. So why did John the Baptist live this way?

Psalm 4:3 says that we have been set apart by God for Himself. God had set John apart for a very special purpose. That means he would be different. He was chosen to tell others about Jesus. God has chosen you to be different too! How has He set you apart?

I know God loves me because He has set me apart as His own.

Know that the Lord has set apart the godly for himself.
Psalm 4:3

God will shelter me from the
storm, just as He sheltered Noah.

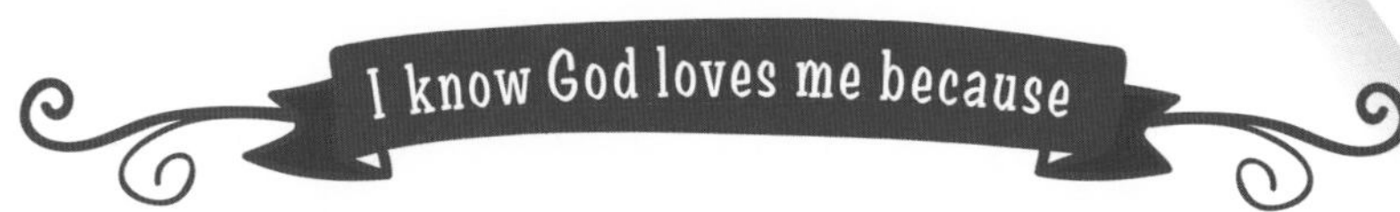

He shelters me from the storm.

GENESIS 6–8

God told Noah a great flood was coming. He told Noah to build an ark, and Noah obeyed. When the ark was finished, God brought all the animals to the ark. When Noah's family and all of the animals were in the ark, the floodwaters came, and God sealed the door to the ark.

Isaiah 25:4 gives us comfort. God promises to shelter us from the storm. The rain fell for forty days and nights. But God had given Noah and his family shelter from the storm. They were safe inside the ark because Noah had obeyed God. So the next time it rains, remember Noah. God will be your shelter too!

I know God loves me because He shelters me from the storm.

You have been . . . a shelter from the storm and a shade from the heat. Isaiah 25:4

God shows me grace, just as
He did to the church at Ephesus.

My Grace Is Sufficient, Child
CD 2 SONG 31

He shows me grace.

EPHESIANS 2:1-10

Paul wrote a letter to a church in a city called Ephesus. He told them, "We are saved by grace." What does it mean to be saved? And what is grace? Paul made it easy to understand.

Ephesians 2:4-8 says that our sin puts us in danger. It causes us to be separated from God. But God loved us so much that He sent Jesus to save us, to rescue us from that danger. God shows us His grace and His favor, by being kind to us, forgiving us, and giving us a life forever with Him.

I know God loves me because He shows me grace.

For it is by grace you have been saved, through faith.
Ephesians 2:8

God will show me how
to live like Jesus.

He shows me how to live.

GALATIANS 5:22-23

Jesus lived "by the nine." *What's that?* you ask. Jesus lived a life pleasing to God, and He wants us to do the same. So how do we please God? We do the things Jesus did; we live "by the nine." Are you ready to try it?

Galatians 5:22-23 shows us "the nine." To live like Jesus we must (1) love others, (2) live with joy, (3) live in peace, (4) be patient, (5) be kind, (6) do good, (7) have faith, (8) be gentle, and (9) have self-control. That's living "by the nine." That's living like Jesus!

I know God loves me because He shows me how to live.

The fruit of the Spirit is love, joy, peace, patience, kindness, goodness, faithfulness, gentleness and self-control. Galatians 5:22–23

God speaks to me
through His Word.

My Word Will Never Pass Away
CD 2 SONG 33

He Speaks to me in His Word.

ROMANS 15:4

Let's think of some ways we can speak to or communicate with each other. We can call someone on the phone. We can send a letter. We can make a video. How about a text message? Or walkie-talkies? Wow! There are a lot of ways to speak to someone. But how does God speak to us?

Romans 15:4 says that God speaks to us through His Word. We call God's Word the *Bible*. God uses the words written in the *Bible* to teach us, to tell us things He wants us to know. So when you ask, "Do You love me, Lord?" His answer is found in Jeremiah 31:3, "I have loved you with an everlasting love."

I know God loves me because He speaks to me in His Word.

For everything that was written in the past was written to teach us, so that through . . . the Scriptures we might have hope. Romans 15:4

God sticks closer than a brother,
just as Jonathan and David did.

Walking with Jesus
CD 2 SONG 34

He sticks closer than a brother.

1 SAMUEL 18:1-4; 19:1-3

Jonathan and David were the best of friends. To show his friendship, Jonathan gave David his robe, his sword, and his bow. In times of danger, Jonathan protected David. They loved each other like brothers. Could there ever be a better friend than that?

Proverbs 18:24 tells us there is a kind of friend who is closer than a brother. Real friends are loyal and love you at all times. And God is our very best friend! He sticks closer than a brother because He's always there!

I know God loves me because He is closer to me than any brother or friend.

There is a friend who sticks closer than a brother.
Proverbs 18:24

God will give me mighty power,
just as He did for Samson.

He strengthens me.

JUDGES 13, 16

Samson was an amazingly strong man! But he had become so weak. He had disobeyed God, and now he stood between two columns at the Philistine temple. He asked God to restore his powerful might. What would God do?

Exodus 15:2 says that the Lord is our strength! God answered Samson's prayer and gave him super strength one last time. When we feel weak and tired, we can ask God to strengthen us too.

I know God loves me because He gives me strength.

The Lord is my strength and my song.
Exodus 15:2

God supports me to keep me
from falling into sin.

He supports me.

PSALM 94:18

Sometimes the road we travel is narrow and steep. When there is ice on the road, it becomes very slippery and dangerous. Even if we walk carefully, we might fall. We need some support!

The author of Psalm 94 wrote that he was about to slip and fall. He wasn't afraid of falling on the ground. He feared he would make a bad choice and fall into sin. But before he did, the Lord brought him comfort and joy. He kept him from falling. Yes, there are many ways we can fall, but the Lord supports us every time!

I know God loves me because He supports me.

When I said, "My foot is slipping," your love, O Lord, supported me. Psalm 94:18

God will calm my fears,
just as He did for David.

He takes away my fear.

PSALM 56:3

David killed a bear that tried to take one of his sheep. And he protected his sheep from wolves day and night. He even fought a giant named Goliath! You'd think David wasn't afraid of anything, right? Wrong.

Psalm 56:3 tells us that David knew what it was like to be afraid. But he found the secret for calming his fear. He decided that when he was afraid, he would trust in God. He knew that God was with him. God can turn our fears into faith, no matter what the fear may be.

I know God loves me because He takes away my fear.

When I am afraid, I will trust in you.
Psalm 56:3

God takes care of me as I sleep
and wakes me up every morning.

I know God loves me because

He takes care of me in the night.

PSALM 3:5

When I'm tired from a busy day, I'm ready for a good night's sleep. I put on my pajamas and brush my teeth. I say my prayers and hop into bed. And before I know it, something very amazing happens. Do you know what it is?

Psalm 3:5 says that we lie down and sleep. Isn't it wonderful to snuggle up in a warm, soft blanket and rest? This Bible verse also says that as we sleep, God is there to sustain us. That means that even as we sleep, God is taking care of us. Then He wakes us up, refreshed, with morning light.

I know God loves me because He takes care of me through the night.

I lie down and sleep; I wake again, because the LORD sustains me. Psalm 3:5

God will take my troubles
and worries from me.

He takes my troubles.

1 PETER 5:7

Have **you** ever played a game called Hot Potato? You place a small ball in your hand, then pretend it's very hot—like a potato hot from the oven. When you try to hold something that is very hot, your hand gets burned. So if you're good at pretending, you pass the ball very quickly to the next person, like it's a hot potato!

First Peter 5:7 is the hot potato verse. It tells us that we can pass our troubles and worries to God—just like a hot potato. How do you do that? You pray, "Lord, I am so worried. But You have promised to take my worries. So now I give them to You." You can play Hot Potato and pass your worries to God!

I know God loves me because He takes my troubles.

Cast all your anxiety on him because he cares for you.

1 Peter 5:7

God doesn't want me to worry. He will provide for me just as He does for the birds.

I know God loves me because

He teaches me not to worry.

MATTHEW 6:25-34

Jesus sat on a hillside teaching a great crowd. Perhaps He saw worried looks on some of their faces. He explained, "Look at the birds. Your heavenly Father takes care of them, doesn't He? Aren't you much more valuable than a bird?"

In Matthew 6:26 Jesus tells us how important we are to God. Jesus doesn't want us to worry about our needs. He wants us to have faith that God will take care of us! Remember, no amount of worry will change what God has planned for you. So always trust in Him to give you what you need!

I know God loves me because He teaches me not to worry.

Do not worry. Matthew 6:31

God teaches me to love others,
just as Jesus taught His disciples.

He teaches me to love others

JOHN 13:34

One of the best ways to learn is to watch and listen to someone who is wise. The disciples who were with Jesus every day listened to Him speak about love and forgiveness. They watched Him care for others. They were learning something we all need to know.

John 13:34 says they were learning to love like Jesus. Jesus wants us to live like Him and to love like Him. How did He live? With a loving heart. And do you know who He loved? That's right—everyone!

I know God loves me because He teaches me to love others too!

As I have loved you, so you must love one another.
John 13:34

God will help me to say "No!"
just as He did for Titus.

I know God loves me because

He teaches me to say "No!"

TITUS 2

Paul wanted Titus to understand how God's grace should affect our lives. So he taught him a lesson about a very small word: the word "No." Paul explained that God's grace helps us say "No!" to the things that displease Him.

Titus 2:11-12 gives us a deeper understanding of how to live right. If we are unkind, unholy, unfaithful, unfriendly, uncaring, or unloving, we displease the Lord. So let's say "No!" to the ungodly and say "Yes!" to what is good. That's real understanding!

I know God loves me because He teaches me to say "No!" to sin.

The grace of God . . . teaches us to say "No" to ungodliness.
Titus 2:11–12

God thinks of me,
just as I think of those I love.

I know God loves me because

He thinks of me.

PSALM 144:3

We often think about people we love. We remember a kind word they said, or maybe we think of a special day we spent with them. The thought of that person makes us happy. Did you know that God is thinking of you?

Psalm 144:3 teaches us that God thinks of those He loves. He cares about us. He remembers a very special prayer you prayed. He thinks of the kindness you showed to a brother or sister. Yes, God thinks of those He loves!

I know God loves me because He thinks of me.

O Lord, what is man that you care for him, the son of man that you think of him? Psalm 144:3

God will give me the desires of my heart,
just as He did for Elizabeth and Zechariah.

I know God loves me because

He will give me the desires of my heart.

LUKE 1:5-25

Elizabeth and Zechariah both wanted a child with all their hearts. They did everything God said to do. But they had no children, and they were both very old. Had God forgotten their prayers? Does God ever forget a prayer?

Psalm 37:4 tells us that God will give us the desires of our heart. But we must ask for things that please God and help others. This story has a happy ending. Though Elizabeth and Zechariah were very old, they became the parents of John the Baptist. He was the desire of their hearts.

I know God loves me because He will give me the desires of my heart.

Delight yourself in the Lord and he will give you the desires of your heart. Psalm 37:4

God promises never to leave me,
just as He never left Joshua.

He will never leave me.

DEUTERONOMY 31:1-8

Joshua was given a big job to do. Moses was stepping down, and Joshua would become the new leader. Moses told Joshua to be strong and brave, and to not be afraid. He said, "God will never leave you nor forsake you." How can we be sure that God will not leave us?

Hebrews 13:5 is a promise that begins with the word *never*. *Never* simply means "not ever." God promised "not ever" to forget Joshua, and He makes that same "not ever" promise to you and me!

I know God loves me because He will never leave me.

Never will I leave you; never will I forsake you.
Hebrews 13:5

God promises that even the bad things that happen will work for my good.

He works for my good.

ROMANS 8:28

Do you want to know one of the greatest promises ever made? Paul relied on this promise. It makes us feel better when nothing else can. What is the promise? All things that happen—no matter what—are working together for our good. But the Bible tells us what we must do before claiming this promise. Do you know what it is?

Romans 8:28 tells us. We must love God. If we love God by serving Him and others, everything that happens to us works for our good. Troubles are never fun, but don't worry. Even times of trouble are working for our good.

I know God loves me because He works for my good.

And we know that in all things God works for the good of those who love him, who have been called according to his purpose. Romans 8:28

God's angels will keep me safe,
just as they kept Daniel safe.

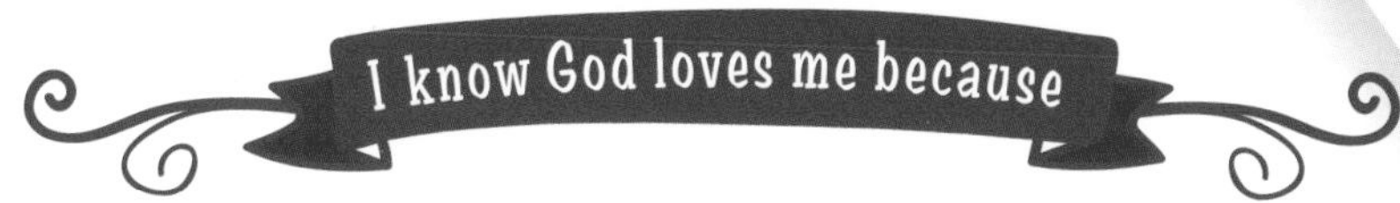

His angels watch over me.

DANIEL 6

Daniel loved God, and he prayed every day. Then the king made a new law: "No more praying!" But Daniel wouldn't stop. So the king's helpers threw him into a den of hungry lions. Who would watch over Daniel?

Psalm 34:7 says that God has placed an angel around those who honor Him. With lions all around, Daniel prayed. And God sent an angel to close the mouths of the lions. Daniel was saved!

I know God loves me because He sends His angels to watch over me.

The angel of the LORD encamps around those who fear him.
Psalm 34:7

God's love for you
and me will never end.

His love will last forever.

PSALM 136:1

Have you ever gone on a vacation? Was it fun? When it was time to leave, did you want to stay one more day? Just imagine if you could go to a place where there was always another day. No matter how long you stayed, there would always be another day. Is there such a place?

Psalm 136:1 says that God's love for you and me lasts forever. No matter how many days He loves us, there is always another day. A vacation may come to an end, but God's love never will. It lasts forever in heaven!

I know God loves me because His love will last forever.

Give thanks to the Lord for he is good. His love endures forever.
Psalm 136:1

God shows me miracles—just as
He showed Noah—to say, "I love you!"

I see His miracles every day.

GENESIS 8-9

The door on Noah's ark opened. Out came animals of every kind. And then a miracle happened: the very first rainbow appeared in the sky! God had stretched a rainbow across the sky as if to say, "I love you!"

Psalm 104 tells of the many miracles of God. There are butterflies and hummingbirds . . . and the rainbow. Its dazzling colors still say, as it did to Noah, "God loves you!"

I know God loves me because He shows me miracles.

You are the God who performs miracles.
Psalm 77:14

God's love for me is
connected like a strong chain.

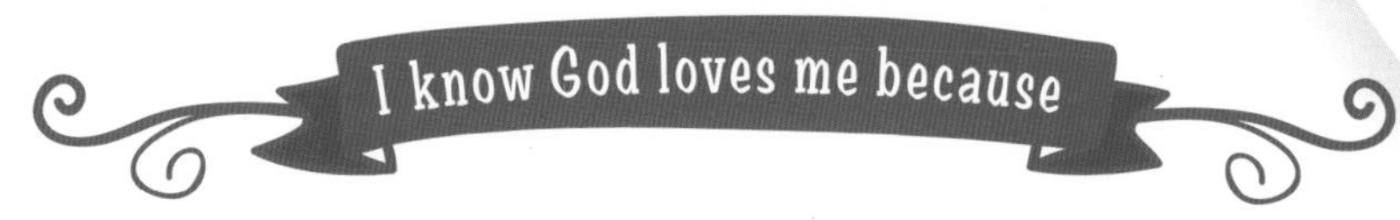

Nothing will separate me from His love.

ROMANS 8:38-39

Paul often sailed the seas in big ships with huge, heavy anchors that helped them stop. Attached to the anchor was a strong chain made of iron. A strong chain was used so that the ship would not break away from the anchor.

Romans 8:38-39 talks about a different kind of chain. Anchor chains can break and separate, but nothing can separate you from God's love. Like the strongest chain ever, Jesus connects your hand and God's hand. And He never lets go! Nothing can ever separate you from God's love in Christ Jesus. That is one chain that will never break!

I know God loves me because I will never be separated from His love.

[Nothing] will be able to separate us from the love of God that is in Christ Jesus our Lord. Romans 8:39